The Ultimate Guidebook for Dog Owners

(from a veterinarian)

The Ultimate Guidebook for Dog Owners

(from a veterinarian)

How to choose, care for, and keep happy, healthy puppies and dogs

Dr. Marlena Lopez BSc DVM

Smith Street Books

Introduction 6

Choosing the Right Breed for You 8
Getting a Dog: What Age is Right for You? 10
Evaluating Sources of Information 12
Pet Insurance 14
Microchips 16
How Often Should Your Dog Visit a Vet? 18
Dogs that Dislike the Vet 20
Why Do Puppies Need So Many Vaccines? 22
Puppy School 24
Crate Training Your Dog 26
Exercise 28
Dog Park Etiquette 30
Dog Vaccines 32
Neutering Male Dogs 34
Spaying Female Dogs 36
What Age to Spay or Neuter Your Dog 38
Common Myths of Desexing Debunked 40
Breeding 42
How to Read a Dog's Body Language 44
Positive Reinforcement Training 46
Ear Cropping & Tail Docking 48
Allergies 50
Fleas, Worms & Other Parasites 52
Ear Infections 54

Holidays & Your Dog 56

Fireworks 58

Alcohol Toxicity 60

Candles & Essential Oils 62

Chocolate Toxicity 64

Grapes, Raisins, Sultanas & Currants 66

Allium Toxicity 68

Poisonous Plants 70

Xylitol Toxicity 72

Dental Care 74

Teething 76

The Importance of Toothbrushing 78

How to Brush Your Dog's Teeth 80

The Benefits of Dental Chews, Diets & Rinses 82

Dental Treats to Avoid 84

Shedding 86

Grooming Your Dog 88

How to Tell if Your Dog is Overweight 90

Exercise & Healthy Habits for Weight Loss 92

The Right Diet for Weight Loss 94

The Risks of Raw Meat Diets 96

How to Recognize Separation Anxiety 98

How to Treat Separation Anxiety 100

Lumps & Bumps 102

Osteoarthritis 104

Saying Goodbye and Remembering your Pet 106

Introduction

Dogs are more than just pets; they are loyal companions, cherished family members, and often, our greatest teachers. Bringing a dog into your home is a life-changing decision, and whether you're welcoming a playful puppy or a wise senior, there's a lot to consider. This book is your go-to resource for navigating every aspect of life with your four-legged best friend.

The Ultimate Guidebook for Dog Owners covers a wide range of topics, from choosing the right breed to understanding the nuances of dog training and health care. You'll learn how to recognize and address issues like separation anxiety, allergies, and dental problems, as well as how to establish healthy routines for weight management and exercise. With practical advice on everything from crate training to reading canine body language, this guide is designed to set you and your dog up for success.

As a veterinarian with a background in general practice and shelter medicine, I've dedicated my career to improving animal welfare and helping pet owners strengthen their bonds with their pets. My work in veterinary clinics has fuelled my passion for educating pet owners, and I have seen firsthand how the right information can transform the lives of dogs and their families. This book is an extension of my mission to empower pet owners with the knowledge they need to build a lasting, rewarding bond with their dogs.

With *The Ultimate Guidebook for Dog Owners*, you'll be well equipped to ensure a lifetime of love, happiness, and health for your canine companion.

1

Choosing the Right Breed For You

Deciding on what kind of dog to get is as important as deciding whether to get a dog in the first place.

Dog ownership is a major commitment of 10-15 years in most cases. If you have done your research and concluded that a dog would be a good pet for your family, and you are willing to meet all that dog's needs, the next step is deciding what dog would suit your lifestyle. To help, here are a few factors to consider.

Your home: It's important to consider the size of your home and evaluate the needs of your family, especially if you have other pets, children, or senior citizens living in the home.

Dog size: Small dogs are more likely to be good lap dogs and adapt well to a smaller home, but they can be more sensitive to colder temperatures. Larger dogs need a bit more space to move around and tend to cost more in terms of food, dog supplies, and medical treatments.

Activity level: Regardless of their breed or size, every dog requires an exercise routine, but some high-energy breeds, such as working dogs or sporting group breeds, enjoy a lot of activity and exercise and require one-to-two hours of moderate activity daily.

Hygiene & grooming: All dogs need basic grooming, however breeds with longer coats require advanced and more frequent maintenance, while short-haired dogs often shed more around the house. Dog breeds with floppy ears have a greater risk of ear infections and may require routine ear cleaning. Smaller breeds are more prone to dental disease and require a dental home care regimen.

2

Getting a Dog: What Age is Right for You?

So, you've decided to get a dog: congratulations! They call dogs man's best friend for a reason – you're embarking on a journey of love and companionship. After deciding what breed suits your lifestyle, you'll need to consider what age will suit your family.

Puppies require a great deal of attention and training, especially over the first six to 12 months. They require toilet training and tend to be more destructive than adult dogs. If you have an active family, a puppy or young dog may be a good choice.

Adult dogs may be a good pick for those who want a dog that's out of the puppy stage and a little bit more relaxed. Adult dogs tend to have been trained and socialized to some degree. Some level of instruction may still be required, though, and any dog will have an adjustment period when you bring them home.

Senior dogs need homes just as badly as younger dogs, and are often more interested in cuddles over exercise. If you and your family lead a relaxed lifestyle, a senior dog may make the perfect companion. By adopting a senior dog, you could save their life. Older dogs can become easily disoriented and anxious in shelters and pounds and are, unfortunately, among the first to be euthanized if they aren't adopted in a timely manner, due to overcrowding.

3

Evaluating Sources of Information

When examining information, it's important to evaluate the reliability of the source, including their education, work experience, and credentials. Veterinary professionals not only undergo extensive education to become licensed, but they are also required to undertake continuing education to learn and discover viable ways to improve on patient care. The best care for your pet is provided as a partnership between your vet clinic and your family.

Social media and the internet can provide pet owners with great information. However, anyone can create a platform and share pet health information, whether they have qualifications or not. Blogs, websites, and social media pages run by laypeople or individuals with no formal nutrition training or education are unreliable resources.

There are some informed and responsible breeders out there, but it's important for pet owners to remember: breeders do not go to veterinary school and should not offer medical advice. A good breeder will have a working relationship with a veterinarian, who will examine the breeder's puppies and give them an initial vaccination, prior to the puppies joining their new family.

Similarly, dog trainers are not legally qualified to prescribe medication. Trainers should always should refer their clients to a veterinarian or veterinary behavior specialist if they believe a dog may benefit from medication.

4

Pet Insurance

Whether it's for humans or animals, the cost of health care is high. Human health care is heavily subsidized by governments and health insurance, concealing the true cost from patients.

Veterinary care is provided by private businesses, which do not receive the same financial support; to take care of pets properly, owners will have to pay veterinary fees that can be difficult to afford.

Pet insurance is designed to protect you and your pet by minimizing the overall cost of veterinary expenses. By agreeing to pay a monthly sum to a pet insurance company, you receive reimbursement for expenses that are covered by the policy.

TIP

Pet insurance helps cover unexpected costs, ensuring your dog gets the best care without financial stress during emergencies.

Insurance will give you peace of mind knowing that you will be financially protected in the event your dog suffers an illness or injury, but it can also help cover the costs of preventative care such as routine check-ups, vaccinations, and dental treatments.

Many pet owners have had to make the difficult decision to euthanize based on financial constraints; insurance will allow you to choose and afford different treatment options and provide life-saving therapies and surgeries.

There is a range of pet insurance providers on the market, and not all policies are created equal. It's important to do your research and compare several different policies to choose one that best aligns with your lifestyle, your dog's breed, and any issues that may arise in the future.

5
Microchips

Microchipping your dog significantly increases the chance of being reunited if they ever become lost.

A microchip is a radiofrequency transponder and a form of permanent electronic identification. The chip itself is only about the size of a grain of rice. It does not require a battery or power and is injected just under the skin between your dog's shoulder blades, in a manner similar to a vaccination. A microchip is not a tracking device; it carries a unique identification number and provides a way for a veterinarian, shelter, or council to contact you if your pet is brought in.

The microchip number is recorded on a database registry with details about the animal and the owner's contact information. It's important for this information to be kept up to date if you move or change phone numbers, so that you will still be contactable should your pet go astray.

Other forms of identification, such as tags and collars, are also recommended. However, they can break off, be removed, or wear out until they are illegible.

Losing your pet can be terrifying. If your dog were to become lost or stolen, knowing that they have a microchip can provide you with some peace of mind and increase the chance of them returning home to you.

6

How Often Should Your Dog Visit a Vet?

Your pet needs regular check-ups to stay healthy, but the frequency of these visits depends on their age, health, and whether they are due for a vaccination. Dogs tend to need more medical attention in the first year of their life and again as they enter their senior years.

In the first year, your dog will likely visit a vet at least four times. Your puppy will need to visit for a series of three vaccinations and to be spayed or neutered. At these visits, your vet will examine your puppy to make sure they're growing well and for any signs of illness.

After your pup has stopped growing and matured socially, they are considered an adult. During this stage of your dog's life, you may only need to visit the vet once a year, depending on their overall health.

Your vet will thoroughly examine your dog from head to tail, recommend dental procedures or administer vaccines if required, and perform bloodwork or other tests to investigate any potential problems. Annual health checks are vital for your dog's health because they allow vets to diagnose, treat, and even prevent problems before they become life-threatening.

For senior dogs, around eight years of age and onwards, twice-yearly check-ups are recommended. In addition to routine vaccinations and health exams, senior pets may require blood and urine tests as they are likely to develop diseases such as arthritis, heart disease, thyroid problems, kidney disease, cancer, and dementia.

7

Dogs that Dislike the Vet

Here are a few tips that can help reduce anxiety around vet visits.

Regular veterinary visits: Regular visits to your veterinary clinic for yearly check-ups ensure that your dog does not just associate the clinic with negative interactions like blood draws or needle injections when they are unwell. Regular visits also help build a relationship between your dog and your vet, so that your dog feels comfortable during physical exams and hospital stays.

Positive reinforcement: Bring along your dog's favorite treats to your vet visits and keep them relaxed by giving plenty of physical attention and talking softly and calmly in the waiting room to create a more enjoyable experience.

Muzzle training: Muzzles are not just for aggression – they can be a safety tool for all dogs and can lower stress at the vet and the groomer's. Training your dog to like a muzzle prior to ever needing one will save both you and your dog stress in the future.

Use of nutraceuticals and pheromones: Use pheromone sprays on a towel you place in the car to reduce stress during transit. Nutraceuticals can be used prior to stressful events.

Medications/sedation when needed: Your veterinarian may recommend behavior-modifying medication or sedation to perform examinations or procedures safely.

8

Why Do Puppies Need So Many Vaccines?

Most puppies will be given their first vaccination at around six to eight weeks of age, before you bring them home, but it is vital to ensure their vaccination certificate confirms this.

Puppies need a total of three vaccinations given four weeks apart due to maternal antibody interference; puppies have temporary protection against many diseases, thanks to the antibodies they receive from their mother's milk within the first few days after birth. However, these maternal antibodies decline within a few weeks, after which puppies need vaccinations to build their own immunity.

While maternal antibodies are circulating in the puppy's system, they can interfere with the way the vaccine works. The exact age that maternal antibodies become ineffective, leaving the puppy vulnerable, is highly variable, ranging from three to 12 weeks. The mom may pass a different number of antibodies to her pups, and these may fade at different rates in each one. Thus, puppies are vaccinated several times to ensure maternal antibodies can no longer interfere with proper immunization, without leaving the puppy susceptible to disease.

The immunity from puppy vaccination weakens over time: your pet will need a booster vaccine. At your dog's annual health check, your veterinarian can advise you on which immunizations are required.

9

Puppy School

Bringing a new puppy home is exciting for the whole family, but it is also a big change for you and your puppy. To build a positive and trusting relationship, and to ensure that the transition goes smoothly, puppy school is recommended. A fun and interactive course, it will help your pup grow into a confident, social, and well-behaved dog, and will equip you with knowledge on basic training, dog behavior, handling, and general care.

Puppies develop vital social and communication skills in the first few weeks of life, which means that puppies should start classes between eight and 16 weeks of age. Puppy school has been shown to improve behavior and prevent future problems like fear of strangers and other dogs. But before they attend, they must have at least one vaccination and a vet check a minimum of two weeks prior to their first group class.

At puppy school, they will learn socialization and communication through play sessions with pups of a similar age group, in a safe and controlled environment. Pet owners will learn how to use reward-based dog training to teach their pups basic cues, initiate lead walking, toilet training, and prevent unwanted behaviors like jumping on people and biting.

If conducted at a vet clinic, puppy school also provides pet owners with an opportunity to seek advice on general care, and should create positive associations with the vet, making future visits a positive experience.

TIP

Puppy school teaches socialization in a safe space, helping pups learn proper interactions before meeting less patient older dogs.

10

Crate Training Your Dog

When you should crate train your dog: Dogs naturally find comfort in enclosed spaces and crates can provide a safe retreat when they feel anxious. Proper crate training, using positive reinforcement, can benefit both puppies and adult dogs, aiding with toilet training and providing a secure environment. Dogs view their crate as their den and avoid urinating or defecating in it, which helps to establish toileting routines. Crates also make transportation less stressful. To ensure crate training is effective, puppies should only be crated for a couple of hours at a time and adult dogs need regular toilet breaks. Crate training should be a gradual and positive process, never rushed nor forced.

When you should not crate train your dog: Crates are not suitable for all dogs and should never replace proper exercise and enrichment. Crate training doesn't address behavioural issues like separation anxiety; in fact, confinement can worsen their distress without resolving the underlying cause. Excessive crating limits physical activity, opportunities for toileting, and will impinge on their social and behavioral needs, impacting their quality of life. Puppies have less control over their bladders and bowels, and crating for long periods can affect their muscle and skeletal development. Crating should only have positive associations as a safe space. Associating punishment and fear with the crate will negate all its potential benefits.

11

Exercise

The amount of exercise your dog needs is influenced by their breed, life stage, and overall health. Most dogs need 30-60 minutes of physical activity each day. Inactive dogs are at risk of becoming overweight, predisposing them to diabetes, heart disease, kidney disease, and exacerbating orthopedic concerns such as hip dysplasia and arthritis.

Toy breeds' need for exercise is often overlooked. While they are great lap companions and can be satisfied spending most of their day indoors, they still require daily exercise of at least 30-40 minutes. High-energy dog breeds such as herding and working dogs have higher exercise needs and crave more rigorous activity. Any flat-faced breeds such as bulldogs and pugs, meanwhile, may have trouble breathing, thus light exercise with frequent breaks is recommended. As a rule, it's not safe to exercise any dog in extremely hot or cold environments, but it is especially important not to take flat-faced dogs outside in hot and humid weather.

On days with extreme weather, you can provide enrichment activities for your dog inside by playing with toys, practicing obedience training, and climbing stairs. Good exercise should be both mentally and physically stimulating, such as exploring a new hiking trail, swimming, or visiting a dog park or doggy day care center.

Exercise is equally important in senior dogs as it is in other stages of life, but seniors may require activities which are less strenuous. If your pet has a pre-existing health condition, talk to your vet for advice on tailored exercise options.

TIP

Seasonal safety: Hot pavement can burn paws in summer. To check if the pavement is too hot for your dog's paws, use the "seven-second test." Place the back of your hand on the pavement for seven seconds. If it's too hot for you, it's too hot for your dog.

12

Dog Park Etiquette

Trips to the dog park are an opportunity to bond, socialize, and run off some pent-up energy. However, all that fun comes with responsibility. On top of individual parks' displayed rules, there are some general etiquette and safety guidelines that pet owners should follow.

Visit the dog park without your dog first to review the park rules and check out the amenities to see if water and poop bags are provided, or if you need to bring them.

Dogs entering a dog park should be fully vaccinated, registered, microchipped, and up to date with parasite protection (such as flea and worming control); puppies who still need to finish their vaccinations are at risk of contracting illnesses from other dogs.

Your dog should wear a collar with identification and be walked using a lead until you reach the off-lead area. Ensure your dog has a good recall around distractions. This will protect them from running out onto a road, getting lost, or entering an altercation with other dogs.

Dog parks aren't suitable for all dogs; do not enter the dog park if your dog has known fears or issues associated with other dogs, or if they show any signs of illness. Don't bring a female dog in heat to the dog park; their presence can create conflict between male dogs.

13

Dog Vaccines

Regular vaccination is an important part of routine canine health care and helps to ensure your beloved companion remains fit and well.

Vaccines work by exposing the body's immune system to a particular part of an infectious agent. This stimulates their immune system to recognize the agent, so that when it is encountered again, the body will mount a rapid and strong immune response to prevent the animal from getting sick.

Core vaccines protect animals from life-threatening diseases that have global distribution and that all dogs, regardless of circumstances or geographical location, should receive. For dogs, these core vaccines protect against canine distemper virus, canine adenovirus, and canine parvovirus. The use of non-core vaccines is determined by geographical location, lifestyle, and exposure risk; these may protect against rabies, leptospirosis, kennel cough, or Lyme disease.

Since vaccines stimulate the immune system, side effects such as allergic reactions, sensitivity to the vaccinated area, fever, or sleepiness may occur. These signs should resolve within a few days; any adverse effects should be discussed with your vet. However, the benefits of protection against diseases outweigh the risks of potential side effects.

14

Neutering Male Dogs

As part of the battle against pet overpopulation, it is widely recommended to neuter male dogs not intended for breeding.

Neutering, otherwise known as castration, reduces unwanted litters and unnecessary euthanasia. Performed under general anesthetic for pet safety and comfort, it involves the removal of the dog's testicles and associated structures, rendering your pet unable to reproduce. Before the surgery, dogs should be given a thorough physical exam to ensure they are in good health.

Removal of the testicles results in decreased testosterone, and consequentially in a reduction of behavioral and health issues. Unneutered male dogs can develop prostate diseases including abscesses and infections, testicular torsion, certain types of cancers; neutering reduces the risk of those diseases.

Neutering is not a quick fix for all behavioral problems in male dogs, but it reduces inappropriate behaviors such as roaming to find a mate, mounting furniture and people, marking inside the home, and engaging in fights with other males. Neutering will not eliminate behaviors that your dog has learned or that have become habitual.

Neutered male dogs tend to live longer than intact males; this relationship's cause and effect has not been established, but it's possible that castrated males are less likely to exhibit risky behaviors, and owners who have presented their pets for castration often continue to present them for consistent veterinary care.

15

Spaying Female Dogs

An ovariohysterectomy, or spaying, is recommended for female dogs not intended for breeding. Spaying reduces unwanted litters and unnecessary euthanasia, and offers health and behavioral benefits.

Performed under general anesthetic for pet safety and comfort, spaying involves the surgical removal of the uterus and both ovaries, rendering your pet unable to reproduce. Before the surgery, dogs should be given a thorough physical exam to ensure they are in good health.

Spaying your female dog before her first heat drastically reduces her risk of mammary, ovarian, and uterine cancers. It also helps prevent the development of pyometra, a life-threatening uterine infection that usually requires emergency surgery.

Spaying stops your dog from having her period and reduces hormonal fluctuations, which are both caused by a female dog's heat cycles. This reduction in hormonal fluctuations results in more predictable behavior and will reduce their desire to escape to find a mate.

It's a common misconception that female dogs should have one litter before being spayed. Unless you intend to breed your dog, there is no need to wait until after your pet has a litter.

Waiting exposes them to the risks of pregnancy and birthing difficulties, while reducing spaying's protective effect against mammary cancer.

16

What Age to Spay or Neuter Your Dog

There is no one-size-fits-all answer to the question of whether to spay or neuter your dog.

Traditionally, most dogs are spayed or neutered at six to nine months. Some clinics and shelters may safely perform these procedures on dogs as young as two months old. However, hormones produced by the reproductive organs in both male and female animals play an important role in the maintenance of body muscle and bone growth. Removing these organs also removes these hormones; because of this, veterinarians may recommend that large-breed dogs prone to orthopedic injury or diseases should be fully grown or have reached sexual maturity before they are desexed.

For female dogs, early spaying significantly decreases the incidence of malignant mammary cancers; because of this, the best recommendation for non-breeding female dogs is to spay prior to their first heat. However, dogs spayed before three months of age have an increased incidence of urinary incontinence, and dogs spayed before six months of age may experience a negative effect on their cranial cruciate ligament. Because of this, spaying after six months of age but before their first heat is most beneficial. However, their first heat, even with knowledge of the family history, can be challenging to predict. Thus, six to nine months is widely accepted.

The decision to spay or neuter, and at what age, is ultimately up to the owner and should be based on the best available evidence. The recommended age for desexing varies between different breeds. Your veterinarian can provide information to help you make an informed decision and determine the best time to spay or neuter your specific pet.

17

Common Myths of Desexing Debunked

Myth: It will cause my dog to gain weight.

Truth: Weight gain is not inevitable in a spayed or neutered dog.

Aging can cause your dog's metabolism to slow, and pets are typically desexed at the same age that their growth starts to slow and they begin to put on weight. However, obesity is controllable with appropriate diet and exercise.

Myth: I don't need to desex my dog if they are mainly kept indoors, or if one of my dogs is desexed.

Truth: An intact dog's drive to find a mate may lead them to escape from home, putting them at risk of injury from a car, person, or another animal, or of getting lost and not returning home. They also tend to become calmer and easier to train when the desire to find a mate is removed.

Myth: It's expensive to have my dog castrated or spayed.

Truth: Compared to the potential risks of not desexing your dog, surgery is inexpensive. The price will depend on the sex, size, and age of the dog, as well as the veterinary practice you visit. However, compared to the costs of unwanted litters, Caesarean section surgery, or treatment for an infected uterus or cancer, the once-off cost to desex your dog is generally much lower.

There are many clinics and animal charities that offer low-cost desexing surgeries to reduce the homeless animal population.

TIP

Desexing doesn't change your dog's personality, however it can reduce unwanted behaviors, help prevent some cancers, and responsibly control overpopulation.

18

Breeding

Are you thinking about breeding your dog? There are important things to consider before making that decision.

Breeding dogs is a time-consuming, expensive, and occasionally heartbreaking endeavor. Responsible breeders need to devote their time to learn as much as possible about the breed, canine health, training, and what to expect during breeding. There is an overpopulation of dogs, with many surrendered to shelters every year; responsible breeders should breed dogs out of a passion to improve the breed's standards, not just to increase its numbers or make a profit.

If you do decide to breed your dog, it is important to be objective. Every dog owner thinks that their dog is the best in the world, but it's important to evaluate your dog's good and bad characteristics honestly. Dogs that are bred should be selected for good temperament and overall health. This requires regular veterinary care, good nutrition, pre-breeding tests, proper exercise, and screening for genetic problems.

Raising puppies is a full-time job. Before weaning, they require a safe, warm, dry place, and need close supervision in case complications arise. After weaning, they require extra feeding, cleaning, training, veterinary care, and a good home.

Learn from others who have gone through the experience and establish a relationship with a veterinarian to learn what to expect during pregnancy and labor, after birth, and how to recognize and respond to an emergency.

19

How to Read a Dog's Body Language

There's no such thing as an aggressive dog, just a dog exhibiting signs of aggression, often stemming from fear. These tips focus on how to evaluate a dog's body language.

Eyes: A fearful dog's eyes may appear rounder than normal. They may show more of the white of their eyes (also known as "whale eye").

Mouth: A tense dog may pull their lips back at the corners or wrinkle their lips at the front of their muzzle to display their teeth. They may drool in the absence of food, yawn, lick their lips, and may also growl.

Ears: A fearful dog's ears may be pinned back. As they become more provoked, their ears may move forward and point toward the subject of interest.

Body posture & tail: A relaxed dog will have a loose stance, their tail in a neutral position. A fearful dog may lean away, tremble, lower their body and head, and tuck their tail. They may freeze or try frantically to escape. A dog displaying aggressive body language may have a tense posture, standing on all four paws or leaning forward, with head raised and tail positioned above spine level. When angry and/or afraid, a dog's hair often stands up, usually starting at the neck and often extending down the back to the tail. A very "floofed up" tail is a sign of a very alert dog who may be about to react aggressively.

20
Positive Reinforcement Training

A child turning in their homework on time and receiving a gold star from their teacher; a boss giving a raise to an employee who went above and beyond; these are examples of positive reinforcement and can be applied to canine learning.

Positive reinforcement-based dog training encourages good behavior by giving dogs a reward (a food treat, verbal praise, or favorite toy) in response to desired behavior, while ignoring unwanted behavior. Dogs are motivated by food and praise. By giving them a reward for doing something you want, they are more likely to repeat that behavior.

When choosing a food reward, choose a treat that your dog places a high value on, that still fits within a balanced diet. If your dog is on a special diet, you can use ingredients or pieces of their food.

Positive reinforcement training can be applied to commands, toilet training, lead walking, and preventing unwanted behaviors, including jumping on people and biting.

In nearly all circumstances punishment of any kind can have detrimental effects, and positive training methods are nearly always better in the long run. Punishment is associated with adverse behavioral consequences such as fear, arousal, and aggression. Punishment may also cause some dogs to become confused and exhibit displacement behaviors such as spinning, tail chasing, chewing, licking themselves, and loss of urine control. Positive reinforcement promotes optimal animal welfare and strengthens the human-companion bond.

21

Ear Cropping & Tail Docking

Cosmetic surgery for dogs may sound strange, but that's exactly what some purebreds undergo shortly after birth.

Ear cropping refers to the practice of reshaping a dog's ears by cutting off the floppy parts. This procedure is often performed under general anesthesia on puppies as young as eight weeks old. The ears are then taped to a hard surface for several weeks while they heal so they stay upright.

Tail docking refers to the amputation of all or part of a dog's tail using a cutting or crushing instrument. Often tail docking is performed by breeders without veterinary training. Tails are usually docked when a puppy is merely days old and is often done without anesthesia or pain relief.

Ear cropping and tail docking are cruel, painful, and completely unnecessary mutilations. Ear cropping does not prevent ear infections, and ear flap injuries are rare; there is no medical justification for either procedure. They are performed for cosmetic reasons only and they hurt, even with pain relief. Dogs use their ears and tails to help us, and other animals, understand how they feel. Without these features, dogs have fewer ways of communicating, and if their emotions are misinterpreted, this may lead to discomfort and expressions of distress.

These elective surgeries have long been routine in certain breeds like Dobermans, German Shorthaired Pointers, Pit Bull Terriers, and Schnauzers. While these practices have been banned in many countries, in others, they continue to be unregulated and pose welfare risks.

22

Allergies

Skin allergies are the number one reason dogs are taken to the vet. Allergies occur when there is an over-reaction or hypersensitivity of the immune system to a particular substance, including proteins from plants, insects, animals, or foods. Normally the immune system protects your dog from infection and disease, but with allergies, the immune system can harm the body.

Signs of allergies include symptoms involving the skin (redness, thickening, and itching leading to patchy hair loss), the respiratory system (coughing, sneezing, wheezing, and discharge from the eyes or nose), or the digestive system (vomiting and diarrhea).

Treating allergies can be tricky. Avoidance is the preferred treatment and ideally, you should prevent your dog from coming into contact, inhaling, or ingesting an allergy-causing substance. However, if your dog is allergic to something like pollen, as many are in the spring, avoidance is rarely possible.

Treating the symptoms sometimes works, especially if the allergies are limited by a short window of time (e.g., pollen in the spring); treatment with anti-inflammatory drugs such as corticosteroids or antihistamines blocks allergic reactions in most cases.

Treating allergies involves long-term management and working with a vet to determine what does and does not work for your dog; this may include referral to a veterinary dermatologist.

It is always best to talk to your veterinarian instead of giving any over-the-counter (OTC) medications to your dog. OTC antihistamines may contain other ingredients, such as decongestants, that are not safe for dogs.

> **TIP**
>
> Any food ingredient can produce an allergy, however proteins like dairy, beef, or chicken are common allergens. Work with your vet to identify triggers and tailor your dog's diet.

23

Fleas, Worms & Other Parasites

Regular parasite prevention is an essential part of good pet ownership. Fortunately, there are many pet parasite preventatives available that will keep you and your pets safe This means there are a lot of options to choose from, but this can also lead to confusion. Which option is best?

There are two categories of parasites to protect your pets against: endoparasites and ectoparasites. Endoparasites are organisms that live inside their hosts, while ectoparasites are organisms that inhabit the host's external surfaces.

TIP

If you choose an easy date – like the first or last day of the month – to administer parasite control, it will help keep your schedule consistent and make it easier to remember.

Endoparasites that affect dogs include heartworm, hookworm, intestinal worms, lungworms, and tapeworms. (Heartworm is transmitted through mosquitoes, which are common in many parts of the world, making it important to have year-round heartworm protection.) Ectoparasites of concern include fleas, ticks, and mites.

For any given parasite, there are several preventative options. Many products treat more than one parasite, but none treats them all, so using combinations of products is common.

These products come in many forms, including a topical or spot-on treatment, which involves applying a liquid to your dog's skin that will spread across their body, localizing in the fatty/oily layer of the skin and fur. Other options include tablets, infused collars, and injections.

Because parasite prevalence varies considerably from one place to the next, it is best to consult with a veterinarian when deciding which of the many preventative products best suits your dog.

24

Ear Infections

Ear infections are common in dogs (especially those with floppy ears or a love of swimming). Inflammation of the outer ear canal, also called otitis externa, is a result of bacterial or yeast infections.

Some dogs won't show overt signs of an ear infection but will have a build-up of wax and discharge in their ears, ranging in color from a light yellow to dark brown or black. Other dogs will show more obvious symptoms: head shaking, scratching their ear(s), an odor, crusts or scabs in or around their ear canal, pain when their ears are touched, or redness and swelling of the ear(s). If your dog exhibits any of these signs, it's important to visit your veterinarian as soon as possible. If an infection of the outer ear isn't treated, it can spread to the middle or inner ear canal and may result in deafness, facial paralysis, dizziness, motion sickness, or imbalance. Ear infections can be extremely painful, and the sooner they are treated, the lower the risk of them spreading.

Prevention is always better than a cure. Excess moisture is a common cause of ear infections, so it's important to dry your dog's ears with cotton swabs after water activities. Dogs with recurrent ear infections may have an underlying cause such as allergies and/or may benefit from using a gentle ear cleaner; your vet can help you develop a long-term solution.

25

Holidays & Your Dog

Holidays like birthday parties, national holidays, New Year's Eve, and religious holidays present risks to your dog. Festive occasions are often marked by an abundance of food, drinks, and party favors that are dangerous to your pets. Being aware and prepared will help to protect your beloved companion on the day.

Food and drink items to keep out of reach include onions, chocolate, grapes, nicotine, and alcohol. These are toxic to your pets and should be stored in facilities they cannot physically access.

Bones can tear or obstruct your pet's intestinal tract, so should be disposed of properly. Poultry bones are especially dangerous as they are more brittle; they can splinter when a dog is chewing on them and cause injury to their gastrointestinal (GI) tract.

Glow jewelry may look cute on your pet; however, the plastic can cause GI obstructions and the glowing contents can cause GI irritation.

Decorations such as bows, confetti, ornaments, ribbons and string, and wrapping paper can cause GI obstructions that often require surgery.

Heat and bodies of water attract mosquitoes and other insects; it's important to use insect repellent that is made for dogs.

Make sure that your dog has an identification tag or registered microchip before the big day, to increase the chances of having them returned home if they escape.

26

Fireworks

Fireworks can be quite frightening to dogs and may cause some animals to flee their home in fear. When it comes to fireworks and your pets, remember P.A.T.S.!

Preparation: If you know that loud noises scare your pet, then consider staying home to comfort them.

Accommodation: Leave your pet at home and indoors, shielded from loud noises. Draw curtains/close blinds to shut out bright flashes. Turn on the radio/TV to drown out the fireworks' noises.

Training: If trained in advance, some dogs can become desensitized to loud noises over time. Condition training is a simple process, but it can take multiple months of playing the recorded sound of fireworks for your pet at an increasingly louder volume. Contacting an accredited pet behaviorist to work with your pets on their fears will help prepare them for the next holiday with fireworks.

Sedation/medication: Your vet may prescribe short-term medication to reduce your pet's anxiety and help them 'forget' their fears associated with fireworks. In milder cases, nutraceutical supplements may help alleviate stress and anxiety. Pheromone diffusers, collars, and sprays can also be used to help soothe dogs. The electric diffusers plug into a wall and emit dog-appeasing pheromones to help them calm down and feel comfortable.

27

Alcohol Toxicity

Products containing ethanol, isopropanol, or methanol can cause alcohol intoxication. We mostly think of alcohol as found in beverages. However, it is also in alcohol-flavored chocolates, auto fuel, fermenting bread dough, fragrances, hand sanitizers, liquid medications, and mouthwashes.

Clinical signs of alcohol toxicity can occur as quickly as 15-30 minutes after ingestion. The most common signs include vomiting, diarrhea, incoordination, lethargy, weakness, and excessive panting or drooling.

In more severe cases, a low body temperature, low blood pressure or sugar, decreased respiratory rate, seizures, tremors, coma, and death may occur.

Dogs are highly susceptible to the effects of alcohol. It is important to contact your veterinarian as soon as possible. Your vet may induce vomiting if ingestion was recent, and your dog is not yet showing clinical signs.

Intravenous fluids can help eliminate the alcohol, provide cardiovascular support, and correct electrolyte abnormalities. Your veterinarian may also offer assisted ventilation, seizure control, and other supportive therapies.

In most cases, the prognosis is good. However, cases may be complicated if liquid is inhaled during vomiting, if other toxic substances are also ingested, or if there are pre-existing health conditions. To keep your dog safe, be aware of your drinks; most dogs ingest alcohol because of unattended beverages. Alcoholic drinks made with milk are especially attractive to dogs.

28

Candles & Essential Oils

Dogs have an incredibly powerful sense of smell, which means that scented candles may have a much stronger impact on them than they do on humans.

Candles with synthetic fragrances may aggravate dogs' existing respiratory illnesses, while some dogs may find these scents to be delicious and consume the candle as a tasty snack. This can result in an upset stomach, vomiting, diarrhea, or worse if the candle contains essential oils.

Essential oils can be very dangerous for dogs, depending on how concentrated they are and what compounds they contain. Some well-known toxic essential oils for pets include pine, eucalyptus, tea tree oil, wintergreen, and mint. Many scented candles contain essential oils and unfortunately neither are regulated; companies may produce them without appropriate quality control, and they may not be required to list the ingredients used.

Symptoms of essential oil ingestion to watch out for include difficulty breathing, drooling, redness around the mouth, vomiting, diarrhea, and behavioral changes including depression, fatigue, and weakness.

It's safest to avoid using essential oils around your pets. Unscented candles made of soy, vegetable, or beeswax may be a safer alternative.

However, the smoke of any candle, scented or not, can be irritating to dogs, especially if they have pre-existing respiratory issues. Any candles should be kept out of your dog's reach and only lit if you are in the room to observe.

LED lights are a great alternative for a flickering light, without the risks of a real flame or essential oils.

29

Chocolate Toxicity

While chocolate is a delicious cure for humans' bad days, it can pose a life-threatening risk to dogs.

Chocolate contains the compound theobromine, which is toxic to dogs at certain doses. The concentration of theobromine varies depending on the type of chocolate; cocoa powder, baking chocolate, and dark chocolate contain higher levels of theobromine compared to milk chocolate. As theobromine toxicity is dose-related, the effect of chocolate ingestion depends on the size of the dog, as well as the amount and type of chocolate consumed.

Clinical signs of chocolate toxicosis usually occur within a few hours of ingestion, but some may be delayed for as long as 24 hours. Initial signs may include increased thirst, vomiting, diarrhea, abdominal distension, and restlessness. Dogs may begin to drool or urinate excessively and have trouble standing or walking. Severe clinical signs include hyperactivity, tremors, and seizures. Toxicity can be life-threatening if left untreated.

Even just a small bit of chocolate, especially dark chocolate, can cause illness. If your pet ingests any amount, you should contact your local veterinarian as soon as possible.

The best way to stop your dog from eating toxins is to take preventative action by keeping dangerous foods out of their reach.

30

Grapes, Raisins, Sultanas & Currants

Grapes and their dried varieties (raisins, sultanas, and currants) are a healthy snack for people, but they present a health threat to dogs.

While a clear toxic dose rate of these fruits isn't established, dogs are more likely to be affected if they ingest large amounts. There also appears to be an individual sensitivity - some dogs are more affected than others. Although grapes are not harmful to all dogs, they have been associated with kidney failure in some, so it's not worth the risk to wait if they've ingested any.

The most common initial symptoms of grape toxicity can occur within 12-24 hours of ingestion; these include vomiting, fatigue, and diarrhea. If these symptoms are left untreated, they can lead to decreased appetite and dehydration. The more severe signs of kidney damage do not appear until days after ingestion - these symptoms include nausea, anorexia, vomiting, diarrhea, an ammonia smell to the breath, belly pain, and increased thirst and urination.

If your dog has consumed grapes, raisins, sultanas, or currants, take them to a veterinarian immediately. The sooner toxicity is diagnosed, the sooner decontamination and treatment can start, keeping your pet safer and the treatment's expenses down.

31

Allium Toxicity

Garlic and onions sizzling in a pan might have an appetizing aroma and delight our taste buds, but they can be toxic to dogs. Onions, garlic, leeks, shallots, scallions, and chives are all part of the Allium plant family and can cause serious medical problems for your dog.

Although mild signs of clinical illness may occur soon after ingestion, the most severe consequences are more likely to take several days to appear.

Mild clinical signs include vomiting, decreased appetite, diarrhea, depression, abdominal pain, and drooling. If dogs consume larger amounts, these vegetables can damage their red blood cells, resulting in anemia.

Anemia occurs when there is a lack of healthy red blood cells to carry oxygen to the body's tissues. It can result in pale gums, elevated heart rate, increased respiratory rate and effort, red-colored urine, weakness, and collapse.

Allium toxicity's damage to red blood cells can also cause kidney damage, presenting as increased drinking, increased or decreased urination, vomiting, and decreased appetite.

If your dog ingests any plant of the Allium family, you should take them to a veterinarian. Early decontamination and treatment reduce the risk of serious effects. If ingestion has occurred within a few hours, your veterinarian may induce vomiting and start supportive care. Since signs of anemia may take several days to appear, a series of repeat bloodwork may be advised. If red blood cell destruction occurs, hospitalized care may be recommended.

32

Poisonous Plants

Several popular plants are poisonous to dogs. These include aloe vera, azaleas, bird of paradise, daffodils, daisies, eucalyptus, lilies, sago palm, and tomato plants, to name a few. Consumption of even small amounts of these plants can cause a range of symptoms from vomiting and diarrhea to serious illness, and even death in some cases. Therefore, it's important to check the safety of any plant before giving your pets access to it.

When it comes to pets, however, there is no such thing as a "safe plant." While the database of knowledge we have on toxic plants is growing each day, all plants should be treated with a healthy skepticism, and you should be vigilant of your pets.

There isn't much scientific evidence supporting the effectiveness of pet deterrent sprays. Positive reinforcement training is the preferred method to teach your dog to stay away from plants that may harm them. Curiosity and boredom may lead your dog to nibble on plants, so it's important that you provide them with enough stimulation through chew toys and enrichment activities.

It's a good idea to know what plants are growing in your yard, and you may consider pet proofing your home to ensure vegetation is out of paws' reach.

If you believe your dog has consumed a poisonous plant, contact your local veterinarian or emergency clinic immediately. It is helpful if you can identify the plant or bring a photo or piece of the plant to your vet.

33

Xylitol Toxicity

Plenty of food items are sugar-free nowadays, which means that a lot of human food may be very dangerous for your dog.

Many sugar-free products contain xylitol, a sugar substitute. Xylitol is popular because it is about as sweet as sucrose but only contains about two-thirds of the calories. Example products include sugar-free gum, candies, breath mints, baked goods, pudding snacks, cough syrup, children's chewable or gummy vitamins and supplements, mouthwash, and toothpaste.

When dogs eat something containing xylitol, the xylitol is quickly absorbed into the bloodstream, resulting in a large release of insulin from the pancreas. This rapid release of insulin causes a rapid and profound decrease in the level of blood sugar (i.e., hypoglycemia). Untreated, hypoglycemia can be life-threatening.

Xylitol does have plaque-fighting properties, which are appealing to humans and can also be beneficial to dogs in pet mouthwashes/toothpaste. These products are purposely designed and contain very small, non-toxic amounts of xylitol, but they need to be used according to the label and stored safely to avoid dogs ingesting a large amount.

When used properly, the small amount of xylitol should not cause poisoning.

If you think your dog has ingested a sugar-free product, check the ingredients to see if the product contains xylitol and, if so, contact your local veterinarian.

34

Dental Care

Dental health is as vital to a dog's wellbeing as it is to human health. Dental disease is one of the most common problems diagnosed in pets: most dogs over the age of three years exhibit some level of dental disease.

This can be prevented by providing a good home care program. The ideal regimen includes daily tooth brushing; other treatments can include the use of clinically proven dental diets, treats, wipes, rinses, and/or gels.

Dental disease can cause bad breath, infection, and pain. It can also lead to serious illness; if left untreated, a gum infection can damage the soft tissue, destroy the bone that supports the teeth, and allow bacteria to enter your pet's bloodstream, making them seriously ill.

Once in the bloodstream, the bacteria can lodge in small blood vessels (most commonly in the liver or kidneys) and cause life-threatening disease. However, in partnership with your veterinarian, good canine dental health is achievable.

Home care is imperfect, and periodically tartar must be properly removed and the teeth's surface polished and disinfected by a veterinarian; this professional cleaning is like human dental treatment.

The tartar is removed from the teeth's surface and the gum line. Periodontal sockets are probed and measured to assess periodontal disease. The enamel is polished, and the mouth is disinfected and sometimes treated with a fluoride sealer or plaque repellent.

TIP

Baby toothbrushes are great for small dog teeth, and flavored dog toothpaste can turn brushing into a treat-like experience.

35

Teething

Just like human babies, puppies are born without teeth. Their baby teeth begin to appear at around three or four weeks of age and start to fall out from four to seven months of age as their adult teeth appear. Your puppy may experience some discomfort during teething – the best way to help is to provide them with soft chew toys. It's important that puppies be supervised any time they are chewing on a toy as no toy is 100% safe.

Signs your puppy is teething include red and inflamed gums. A mild amount of bleeding may occur. You may find their puppy teeth on the floor, although puppies will more commonly swallow them, which is normal and safe.

Don't reward unwanted behavior; if your puppy chews on your hands or household items, offer them a toy. At each puppy exam and at the time of spaying or neutering, your vet will assess your puppy's teeth and look for problems such as crooked teeth, jaw misalignment, fractured teeth, and retained baby teeth leading to overcrowding.

When your puppy is teething, it is a good time to get them used to having their mouth touched and examined. Make it a positive experience by offering treats each time you touch your puppy's mouth. This will allow you to introduce a dental care routine early that they will enjoy or at least tolerate.

36

The Importance of Toothbrushing

Plaque is a colorless film of bacteria that constantly forms on teeth. If not removed, this film of bacteria will harden to form tartar. Tartar is usually yellow to brown in color and requires professional dental cleaning to remove.

The best defense against plaque, which results in bad breath and inflammation of gums and the bone that supports the teeth, is regular dental exams and cleaning by a veterinarian, coupled with daily toothbrushing: the gold standard for dental care in dogs. Ideally toothbrushing should be performed daily to reduce plaque build-up.

It can be challenging to make time but turning a dental care routine into a daily habit will make it feel less daunting. When done correctly, toothbrushing can be a positive, bonding experience for you and your pet.

It's best to gradually introduce your dog to having their teeth brushed when they are a puppy so that they become accustomed to the routine. However, older dogs can also learn new dental care routines.

Brushing provides the benefits of mechanically removing plaque from your dog's teeth, as ingredients in the toothpaste kill bacteria.

To get started, you need a toothbrush or finger brush, ideally one designed for dogs, and pet toothpaste. It's recommended to brush your dog's teeth for 30-60 seconds on each side.

37

How to Brush Your Dog's Teeth

To introduce a dental routine, choose a time and place where your dog is calm. For the first few sessions, start by giving their muzzle a light rub with your finger. Advance to lifting their lips and gently touching and then rubbing the outside of their teeth and gums for 15-60 seconds until they become comfortable with you touching the inside of their mouth.

Once your dog is comfortable with you touching their teeth, offer them some dog toothpaste from your finger. Don't use human toothpastes: they contain ingredients that can be toxic to dogs. Dog toothpaste comes in a variety of flavors such as chicken, beef, and mint that are designed to be tasty and appealing to dogs.

The next step is to start using a toothbrush. Toothbrushes designed for dogs have angled handles, are smaller, and have softer bristles; toddler toothbrushes can be used for small breeds.

Start with the easy-to-reach teeth at the front of the mouth, until you both become more comfortable with the process. Then you can move on to the rest of the mouth, brushing all surfaces of their teeth. Stop immediately if there is any sign of aggression.

To make the experience enjoyable, reward your dog with praise and a dental treat or favorite toy afterwards.

38

The Benefits of Dental Chews, Diets & Rinses

The goal of dental chews is to clean your dog's teeth while providing environmental enrichment. Dental chews work by mechanically removing plaque, and some are chemically formulated to create a protective barrier on the surface of the teeth. Dental chews are a great addition to your dog's daily oral care routine, but they should not replace brushing and regular professional cleaning.

A variety of dental chews claim to improve dental health; the Veterinary Oral Health Council is an independent body of veterinary dentists that critically analyzes claims and puts its seal of approval on products designed to reduce plaque and tartar.

Beyond choosing from approved dental chews, it is important to choose chews appropriate for the size and personality of your dog. If the chew is too small, your dog will consume it too quickly for it to be effective, and too many chews in a day quickly add up in calories. If your dog is an aggressive chewer, chew toys, although not edible, can provide a good option for dental health and enrichment.

Some specially formulated dental diets are made of larger kibble that ensure your dog chews through each piece, rubbing the kibble against their teeth with a brushing effect.

Other great options are dental rinses and water additives, which coat the entire mouth including the gums, tongue, and teeth, reducing plaque and freshening the breath. However, like dental chews, these are a great addition to your dog's daily oral care routine, but should not be used in lieu of toothbrushing and regular professional cleaning.

39

Dental Treats to Avoid

Not all dental treats are created equal – some chews are too hard and may seriously threaten your dog's dental and overall health. Other treats are high in fat and pose a risk of bacterial contamination. All treats should be closely moderated.

There are risks associated with providing dogs with bones to chew. Cooked bones are often too hard and may cause tooth wear, or tooth and jaw fractures when there is already disease present. Raw bones are softer, but they can splinter into sharp pieces that cause trauma, and they can become contaminated after lying on the ground at room temperature for prolonged periods. Bones, both raw and cooked, pose the risk of gastrointestinal perforation or obstruction. When choosing dental chews for your dog, there is a general rule to follow: if the chew is too firm to indent with your fingernail, then it's too firm for your dog's teeth.

Hooves and deer antlers are also too firm to be effective chews and can cause digestive tract blockages, vomiting, diarrhea, or choking hazards. They can also break into sharp fragments that can perforate the gastrointestinal tract.

Rawhide chews are made from the skin of cows. They are associated with bacterial contamination, digestive distress, and choking hazards, and are not easily digested, generally. When large chunks are broken off and ingested, they pose a high risk of intestinal obstruction.

Dried pig ears are high in fat and can lead to abdominal discomfort and pancreatitis if not moderated.

The purpose of regular dental chews is to keep your dog's teeth as clean as possible. Brushing is the most effective way to keep teeth clean, and there are no dental chews that work perfectly. Most humans brush twice daily and visit the dentist at least once a year. Dental chews will help, but your dog's teeth still need regular brushing and dental check-ups with your veterinarian.

40

Shedding

There is no such thing as a "hypoallergenic" dog breed. Some shed less than others, leading to less fur build-up in the home – at some point, this became synonymous with "hypoallergenic." While these breeds are not free of allergens, they may spread them less and therefore may be more suitable for people with allergies. However, while some people may be allergic to dog hair, others may be allergic to dog dander or saliva.

All dogs shed their fur – some shed constantly, some shed seasonally, and others don't shed much in comparison, but it's important to understand that all dogs will shed. This is a completely natural process that occurs when dead hair is released to make room for new hair to grow. Dogs shed in preparation for seasonal weather or because of diet changes, and stresses like giving birth, travel, allergies, malnutrition, trauma, or illness.

You can try to limit exposure to dog allergens through environmental controls. Appropriate flea prevention will stop your dog from scratching their skin and releasing dander. Regular brushing of your dog's coat will remove any loose hair in a controlled way, before it spreads across the house. Non-carpeted floors tend to hold less allergens and frequent vacuuming can help remove them. You can also keep your dog out of your bedroom, in addition to using air filters.

41

Grooming Your Dog

Grooming improves a dog's appearance and can help improve their overall health and wellbeing. Grooming on a regular basis will help keep their hair and skin in good shape and provide you with the opportunity to check for parasites (such as fleas and ticks), lumps and bumps, and changes to their weight.

How often you need to brush and bathe your dog will vary depending on an individual dog's needs. Brushing helps to distribute the skin's natural oils through the hair, promoting a shiny coat while removing loose hair and preventing matting. Dogs with long or double coats (e.g., Golden Retrievers) or those with dense coats (e.g., Siberian Huskies) generally need to be brushed on a weekly basis to remove tangles and prevent knots. Dogs with short, smooth coats (e.g., Beagles) can generally be brushed once every few weeks.

Dogs should be bathed when they emit an unpleasant smell or if they have accumulated dirt on their coat. A dog's skin is very different from human skin, including functioning at a different pH level, so human shampoos, even so-called "mild" ones are not at all appropriate for use on dogs. Dogs with skin problems may require a customized bathing schedule and medicated shampoo as part of a treatment plan prescribed by your veterinarian.

42

How to Tell if Your Dog is Overweight

Obesity in pets is a crucial issue – overweight animals are at increased risk of developing serious weight-related disorders such as diabetes, arthritis, high blood pressure, kidney disease, cancer, and more.

To monitor your dog's weight at home, here is an easy trick: With your palm facing down, grip your hand into a fist, then use your other hand to feel the top of your knuckles. You will easily be able to see the bump of each knuckle and grasp around them. If this is what your dog's ribcage feels like, then they are likely too thin.

Now lay your hand out flat and look at your where your knuckles would be – you won't see the big bump of each knuckle anymore, but you can easily feel them without excess fat on top of them. If your dog's ribs feel like this, they are an ideal body weight.

Now flip your hand palm up and feel your knuckles. They're a little more difficult to feel now, but if you press harder, you'll feel a layer of fat over them. If your dog's ribcage feels like this, they are starting to put on a bit too much weight.

If you feel the palm of your hand, there are no knuckles there at all – all you can feel is cushion. This is what the ribcage of a dog that is obese will feel like.

If you're concerned about your pet's body weight, you can visit your veterinarian for a professional weight assessment.

43

Exercise & Healthy Habits for Weight Loss

Exercise is a great way to help your dog stay fit and healthy. Most dogs require 30-60 minutes of physical activity each day, but for overweight dogs, they may need to start out a bit slower with 10-15-minute walks until they build up their fitness. (To put less pressure on their joints, swimming is a great option.)

By making activities fun and exciting, your dog will start to look forward to exercising. Toys and balls can be used to encourage games of chase or fetch – try to play for 10-15 minutes twice a day and reward them with lots of praise.

You should aim for your dog to steadily lose weight over an appropriate length of time through developing healthy habits. If your dog loses too much weight too quickly, this can result in nutritional deficiencies and health issues. The desired weight loss for dogs is one to two percent of their total body weight per week until they reach their ideal weight.

If you get the diet and exercise levels right, your dog should start to gradually trend toward their ideal weight. Unexpected weight loss or gain, especially if accompanied by other changes such as reduced energy, could be an indication of underlying disease.

44

The Right Diet for Weight Loss

Diet plays a vital role in weight loss. To help your dog, it's important to establish a consistent feeding routine; have the same family member feed them each day, for a better chance at this.

Feed your dog their total daily intake over two or three meals throughout the day, rather than one meal – using a slow feeder or puzzle feeder will slow down ingestion and help them feel fuller after mealtimes.

Finally, reduce the amount of treats they are given each day; the calories can quickly add up.

Weight loss is based on the principle that energy expenditure must be greater than caloric intake, so it may seem like a good idea to simply reduce your dog's food. However, this is not recommended: it can encourage poor behavior like aggression or begging and may result in nutritional deficiencies. Veterinary prescription diets are formulated to help your dog lose weight; they generally contain high-quality protein for fat metabolism and energy, and high fiber and low carbohydrate content to help your dog feel fuller with a reduced caloric intake.

When introducing a new diet to your dog, allow about a week to transition by adding a small amount of the new food and subtracting an equal amount of the old food each day; this will minimize digestive upsets.

45

The Risks of Raw Meat Diets

Negative feelings about commercial pet foods, flashy marketing, and anecdotes from friends lead some pet owners to feed their dogs raw food diets. Many pet parents have heard that raw foods are a cure-all for health concerns ranging from allergies to dental problems, arthritis, flatulence, and even cancer. However, there is ample evidence of nutritional deficiencies from raw diets, and contamination of raw food with bacteria and parasites. Raw meats are often contaminated, even if intended for human consumption, which puts your pet at risk - it is assumed people will cook their meat, making reasonable levels of contamination for human food acceptable.

Prior to the widespread availability of nutritionally complete and balanced dog foods in the last four decades or so, it was common for dogs to experience some kind of nutritional deficiency; vets working in the 1950s commonly saw rickets, a disease caused by calcium deficiency.

These days a vet can work their whole career and not see a single case of rickets; this is just one of many nutritional diseases that have become rare since the widespread use of good-quality commercial pet foods.

A thorough understanding of canine nutrition (which is not the same as human nutrition) is needed to ensure that raw meat and whole food diets are balanced and complete. The side effects of getting it wrong can be serious diseases, deformity, or premature death for your dog.

The manufacturers of the leading premium dog foods invest heavily in research and development. They have vast amounts of data, and the leading veterinary bodies around the world all endorse their findings.

46

How to Recognize Separation Anxiety

Does your dog get nervous when you're getting ready to leave the house? Do they destroy your shoes, furniture, or upset your neighbors by barking when you're away? Your dog may have separation anxiety.

Separation anxiety is triggered when a dog that is hyper-attached to their owner becomes distressed when left alone.

This behavior may result from changes in their environment that trigger feelings of distress. This may include a change in the guardian or family structure; dogs adopted from shelters may exhibit anxiety after being abandoned or surrendered. Losing a household member from death or a move can also be a trigger, as can an abrupt change in schedule, like an owner starting to work at an office when they previously worked from home.

Symptoms may include barking and howling, urinating in the house even though they are toilet trained, pacing, drooling, or panting more than usual, and destructive behavior such as chewing and digging. To rule out medical causes for inappropriate urination, visit your veterinarian; it is important to rule out any medical issues before starting behavior modification training.

47

How to Treat Separation Anxiety

Mild cases of separation anxiety may resolve with counter-conditioning training, a technique used to change an animal's emotional responses toward a stimulus from fearful to relaxed.

In cases of separation anxiety, counter-conditioning training focuses on reducing distress when a dog's parent leaves the house. This can be achieved by offering food activities, such as puzzles or treat-filled chew toys, that will take the dog at least 20-30 minutes to finish. This approach only works by itself for cases of mild anxiety, as highly anxious dogs won't eat when left alone.

Severe cases are more complex and often require the use of counter-conditioning and desensitization. To help these highly anxious dogs overcome their fears, consultation with a trained and experienced professional is recommended. A certified animal behaviorist or a board-certified veterinary behaviorist can provide guidance on designing and implementing a desensitization and counter-conditioning training plan.

Medications may also help in severe cases of separation anxiety. A veterinarian or veterinary behaviorist may prescribe anti-anxiety medication to help a dog tolerate some degree of isolation.

It's important to remember: behavior stemming from anxiety is not committed out of disobedience or spite. These dogs are distressed and trying to cope in an anguishing situation.

You should never punish an anxious dog, as it may cause them to become even more fearful and exacerbate the problem. If left untreated, mild anxiety disorders can become more serious over time, and usually mild separation anxiety is easier to manage than chronic, marked separation anxiety. Separation anxiety is NOT something your dog will "just grow out of."

48

Lumps & Bumps

Petting your dog is more than just a way to show affection, it's a chance to check for any unusual lumps or bumps. Catching changes early can have a big impact on your dog's health.

When petting your dog, gently run your hands over their entire body, including areas often overlooked, such as the belly, armpits, groin, tail base, and behind the ears. Use your fingertips to feel beneath the fur for any unusual bumps. These can vary in texture, ranging from soft to firm or hard, and may be as small as the size of a bug bite or much larger.

If you find a lump, don't panic. Begin by keeping a detailed record to share with your veterinarian. Jot down when you first notice it, how big it is (using a ruler or measuring tape), and where it's located. Be as specific as you can, for example, "on the right side of the chest, close to the armpit." Over time, keep an eye on it, and note any changes like growth, changes in shape, or signs of redness or irritation. This information will be incredibly helpful for your vet.

Many lumps feel similar, whether they are benign (noncancerous) or malignant (cancerous); because of this, it's important to have them checked out by a veterinarian.

Your veterinarian might begin by performing a fine-needle aspiration, where a small sample of cells is taken from the lump and examined under a microscope to assess whether they appear normal or concerning. While this can give valuable insights, a needle sample only captures a small area and doesn't reveal its full structure or how far it may have spread.

If more investigation is needed, your vet might recommend a biopsy, which involves taking a larger tissue sample or even completely removing the lump for analysis. By staying attentive to changes in your dog's body and seeking prompt veterinary care, you can help ensure their health and well-being.

49

Osteoarthritis

Osteoarthritis (OA), a chronic degenerative condition, is a leading cause of discomfort and mobility issues in dogs. It occurs when the cartilage protecting joint bones deteriorates, leading to inflammation, pain, and restricted movement. Commonly affected joints include shoulders, hips, elbows, and knees. Symptoms range from limping and stiffness to behavioral changes like irritability. While any dog can develop OA, factors like elbow or hip dysplasia often predispose certain breeds.

Diagnosis & prevention: Diagnosing OA involves physical exams and imaging such as X-rays. Early detection is crucial to managing the condition effectively. Prevention focuses on maintaining a healthy lifestyle through proper diet, weight control, and joint supplements. Weight control is paramount in preventing and managing OA. Excess body weight adds undue stress to joints, exacerbating inflammation and pain. Regular, low-impact activities like walking and swimming can support joint health, improve muscle tone, and delay disease progression.

Supplementation for joint health: Dietary supplements can help in the prevention and management of OA. Chondroprotective agents like glucosamine, chondroitin sulfate, and MSM all support cartilage repair and reduce inflammation. While these supplements take weeks to show results and effects may vary, they can be an integral part of a long-term management plan. Omega-3 fatty acids, derived from fish oils, provide additional

anti-inflammatory benefits, helping to alleviate clinical symptoms. Green-lipped mussel is another beneficial supplement, offering anti-inflammatory properties and joint support, making it a valuable addition to OA management strategies.

Therapies & medications: Effective OA treatment typically involves a multimodal approach – a combination of therapies tailored to address various aspects of the condition. This approach integrates medication, physical therapy, and lifestyle adjustments to maximize comfort and mobility. Non-steroidal anti-inflammatory drugs (NSAIDs) are commonly prescribed to manage pain and inflammation. Other therapies, such as specialized injections, cannabinoids, acupuncture, and laser therapy, may provide additional comfort and improved mobility.

Creating a comfortable environment: Adapting your home to suit an arthritic dog's needs is essential. Provide soft bedding, easy access to food and water, and assistive ramps to minimize strain on joints. Regular veterinary check-ups ensure the treatment plan evolves with your pet's changing needs.

Although there is no cure for OA, consistent care, a tailored management plan, and a supportive environment can significantly enhance your dog's quality of life. Always consult your veterinarian to customize treatments and strategies for your pet's specific condition.

50

Saying Goodbye & Remembering Your Pet

Caring for a dog means preparing for all stages of life, from raising a puppy to tending to an aging or unwell senior.

Determining the right time to pursue euthanasia can be tremendously difficult for pet owners, but your veterinarian can work with you to assess your pet's quality of life. If your dog's problems are treatable, early intervention can reduce suffering, and many signs of old age, like arthritis, can be relieved. When other means of alleviating pain and distress are no longer helpful and your pet's quality of life is affected, however, a veterinarian may recommend euthanasia, which is a humane way of inducing death.

> **TIP**
>
> Everyone grieves differently; allow yourself time and space to process loss in a way that feels right for you.

Assessing your pet's quality of life is subjective and depends on your dog's disease progression, their personality and comfort, and your personal beliefs. Pain and anxiety are two of the most important aspects of veterinary hospice care. Persistent and incurable diseases, inability to eat or maintain personal hygiene, difficulty breathing, and lack of interest in activities previously considered enjoyable may be indications that euthanasia should be considered.

Losing someone you love is devastating and it's important to allow yourself to grieve. We all respond to loss differently; you may want to consider engaging in self-care activities, or in mourning practices such as creating a memorial, photo album, or video collage, and talking to others who relate and can help you through the grieving process.

It's never easy to lose a pet, but it is possible to find peace after loss and to reflect on the memories you shared that will forever live in your heart.

Published in 2025 by Smith Street Books
Naarm (Melbourne) | Australia
smithstreetbooks.com

Distributed outside of ANZ, North & Latin America by
Thames & Hudson Ltd., 6–24 Britannia Street, London, WC1X 9JD
thamesandhudson.com

EU Authorized Representative: Interart S.A.R.L.
19 rue Charles Auray, 93500 Pantin, Paris, France
productsafety@thameshudson.co.uk; www.interart.fr

ISBN: 978-1-9232-3911-1

All rights reserved. No part of this book may be reproduced or transmitted by any person or entity, in any form or means, electronic or mechanical, including photocopying, recording, scanning or by any storage and retrieval system, without the prior written permission of the publishers and copyright holders.

Smith Street Books respectfully acknowledges the Wurundjeri People of the Kulin Nation, who are the Traditional Owners of the land on which we work, and we pay our respects to their Elders past and present.

Copyright text and design © Smith Street Books
Copyright illustrations © Hannah Naughton

Publisher: Paul McNally
Editor: Lucy Grant
Text: Dr. Marlena Lopez
Design, illustrations and layout: Hannah Naughton
Proofreader: Pamela Dunne

Text in this book previously appeared in *Coaching Cards for New Dog Parents*.

Printed & bound in China by C&C Offset Printing Co., Ltd.

Book 394
10 9 8 7 6 5 4 3 2 1